NATIONAL GEOGRAPHIC

Ladders

SYMBOLS OF Liberty

AMERICAN WONDERS

GENRE Reference Article

Read to find out about the National Mall in Washington, D.C.

THE National Mall

by Sheri Reda
illustrated by Eric Larsen

The National Mall in Washington, D.C., isn't a patriotic shopping center. It's a long, grassy park that is lined with trees and museums. The Mall is a great spot for parades and political events. It's also where you can see some of the most famous American **monuments**. These monuments that honor important people and events in American history are powerful **symbols** of liberty. They represent the ideals that Americans have fought for throughout history.

The Lincoln Memorial was completed in 1922. It has 36 marble columns: one for each of the states in the Union when Lincoln died in 1865.

Lincoln Memorial Reflecting Pool

The Reflecting Pool lies between the Lincoln Memorial and the Washington Monument. It is more than 2,000 feet long but less than three feet deep.

The Martin Luther King, Jr. Memorial, cut from an enormous single block of solid stone, is the Mall's newest monument and a tribute to a national hero.

Martin Luther King, Jr. Memorial

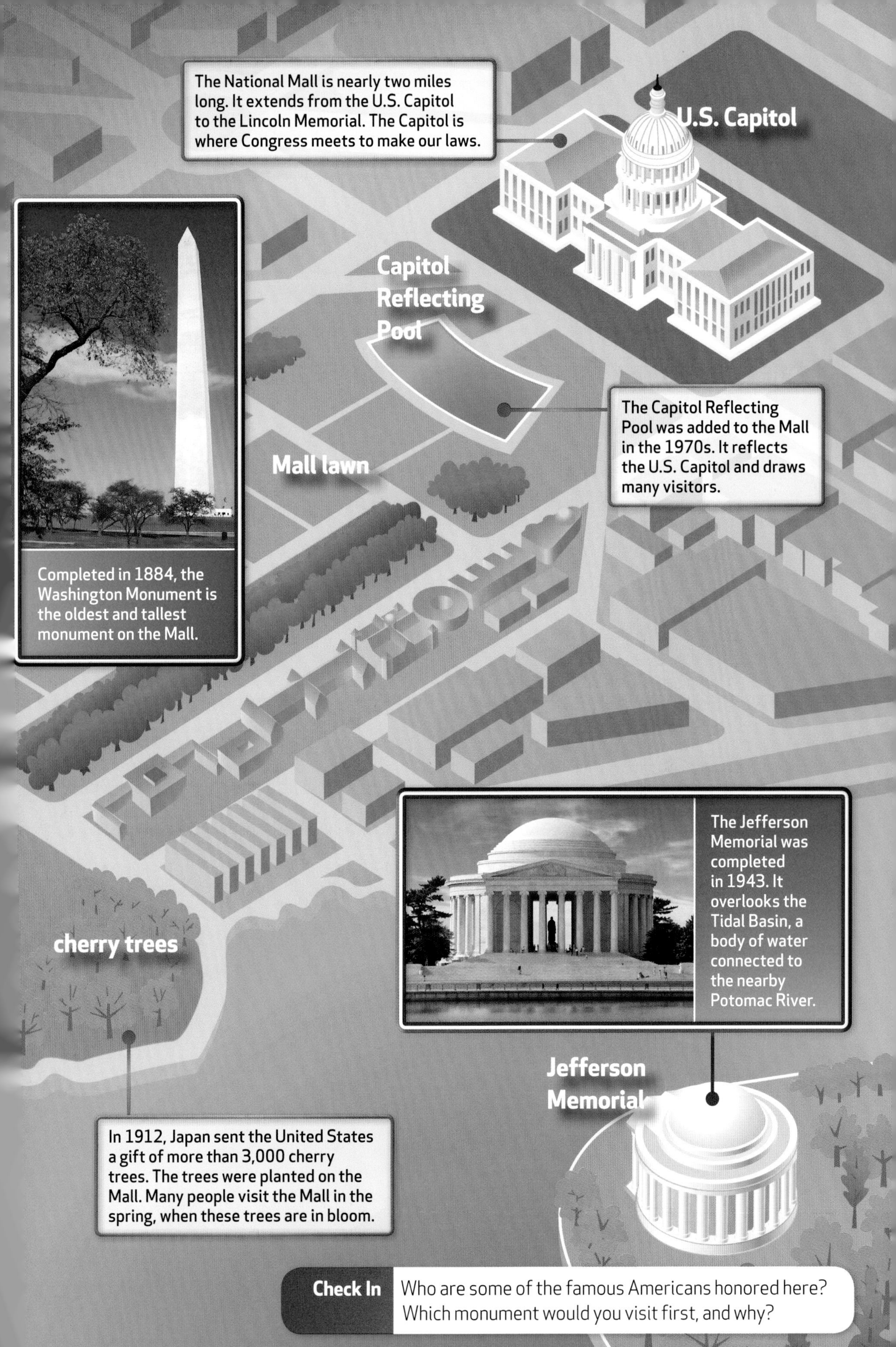

The National Mall is nearly two miles long. It extends from the U.S. Capitol to the Lincoln Memorial. The Capitol is where Congress meets to make our laws.

Completed in 1884, the Washington Monument is the oldest and tallest monument on the Mall.

The Capitol Reflecting Pool was added to the Mall in the 1970s. It reflects the U.S. Capitol and draws many visitors.

The Jefferson Memorial was completed in 1943. It overlooks the Tidal Basin, a body of water connected to the nearby Potomac River.

In 1912, Japan sent the United States a gift of more than 3,000 cherry trees. The trees were planted on the Mall. Many people visit the Mall in the spring, when these trees are in bloom.

Check In Who are some of the famous Americans honored here? Which monument would you visit first, and why?

GENRE Social Studies Article **Read to find out** about the Washington Monument.

A MONUMEN[TAL] Earthquake

by Sheri Reda

Stand next to the Washington Monument and look up. You might wonder if the top pierces the sky. Tourists can't miss the monument. At almost 555 feet tall, it towers over the National Mall to honor our first president—George Washington.

The monument is a fitting tribute to a great leader. George Washington was appointed the head of the American army shortly after the American Revolution began. This was a war between the colonies and Great Britain. Fighting broke out in 1775. Later, Washington was elected president of the newly formed nation. He served two terms as the country's leader.

On any ordinary day, hundreds of tourists can be found roaming the grounds of the Washington Monument. Visitors can climb the tower's 897 steps or take an elevator to the top, where they can take in views of the Mall, the White House, and Washington, D.C. They can even see the states of Maryland and Virginia in the distance. However, on the afternoon of August 23, 2011, tourists felt the tower begin to rattle and shake. Small pieces of stone fell from the ceiling. Tourists looked up, startled and confused. Was it the wind? Was it an accident?

It was an **earthquake**, a violent movement in Earth's crust. The quake shook the entire East Coast, including Washington, D.C.

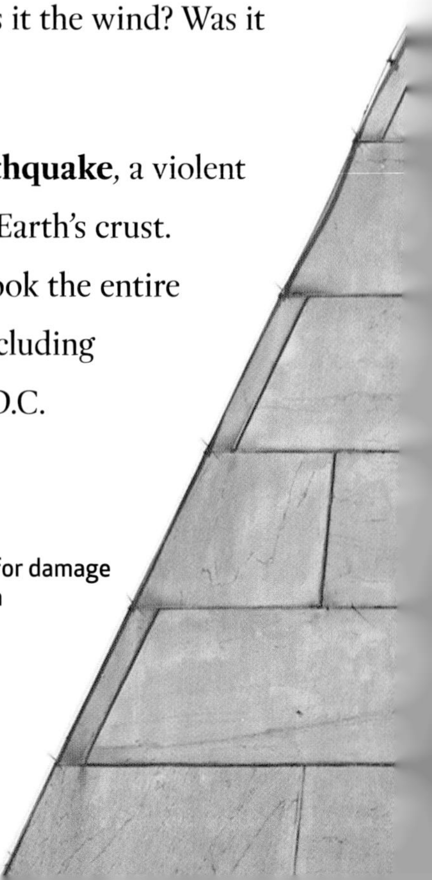

Inspectors check for damage to the Washington Monument after the earthquake.

TAL

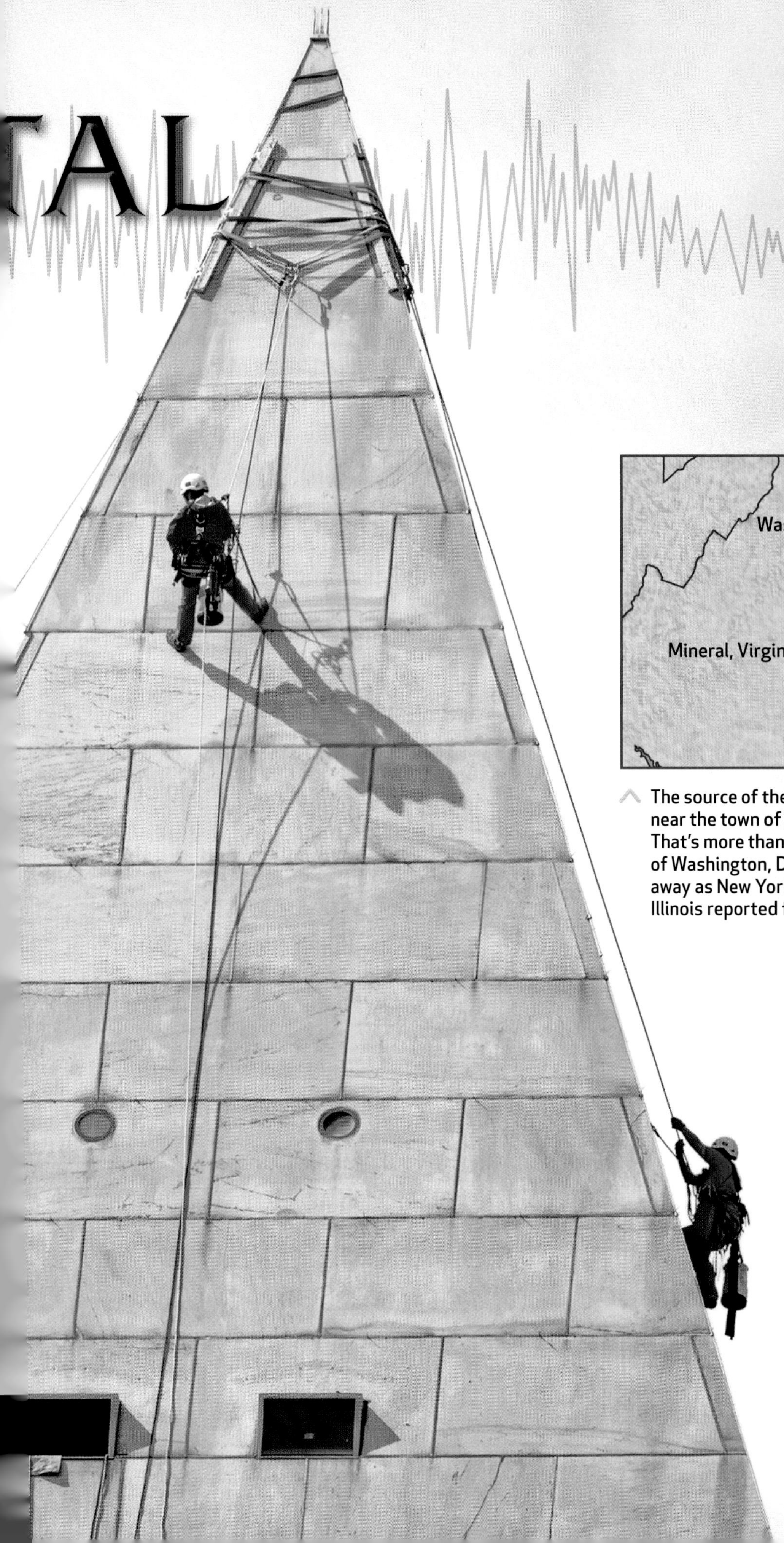

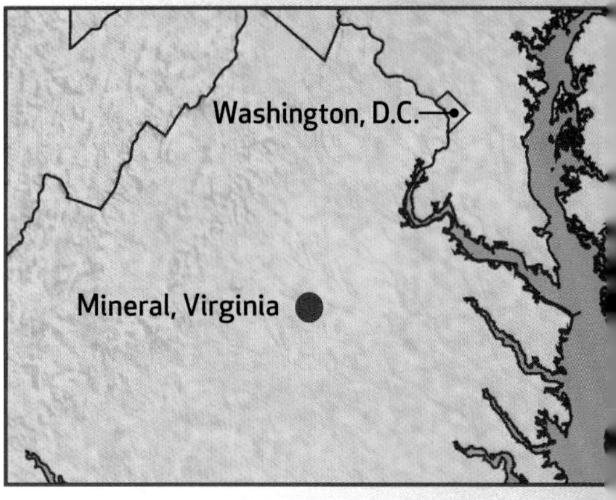

The source of the earthquake was near the town of Mineral, Virginia. That's more than 80 miles southwest of Washington, D.C. People as far away as New York, Georgia, and Illinois reported feeling the quake.

The Damage Done

National park rangers serve as tour guides for the people who visit the monument. The rangers quickly began to evacuate tourists, leading them out of the structure and away from danger. Their efforts were successful. No one was hurt.

After the ground stopped shaking and the dust settled, the tower was carefully inspected for damage. Experts started at the top of the monument and **rappelled** (ruh-PEHLD) down the outside to examine each stone block. Several of the blocks were damaged. Six blocks at the top had large cracks, and the **mortar** between the blocks was broken in many places. Based on the amount of damage they found, the inspectors declared that the building was unsafe. They closed it to the public until repairs could be made.

Workers balance on metal scaffolding as they repair and strengthen the monument after it was damaged by the earthquake.

The earthquake that rocked the Washington Monument was strong enough to crack the building and break off this chunk of marble.

FACTS ABOUT THE WASHINGTON MONUMENT

- The Washington Monument's 36,491 white granite stone blocks weigh just a bit more than 81,000 tons in all, and the foundation weighs another 20,000 tons.
- The monument is a traditional Egyptian **obelisk** (AH-buh-lisk), a tall, four-sided tower with a pyramid at the top.
- The monument is the tallest freestanding stone building in the world.
- The walls are 15 feet thick at the base, but only 18 inches thick near the top.
- Not everyone liked the final design for the Washington Monument. Architect Robert Mills's design had more decoration. He thought that the monument would look too plain. He said it would look like an asparagus stalk.

Built to Last

The damage to the Washington Monument could have been worse. Thankfully, the workers had taken their time to carefully and securely construct the stone tower. In fact, it took more than 40 years to build it. Construction on the tower began in 1848, but a few years later, work stopped due to a lack of funds. Then, with only one-third of the monument complete, the Civil War began. That delayed construction even further. At 156 feet tall, the unfinished monument looked more like a chimney than a grand tower. Finally, the tower was completed in 1888. Many people came to Washington, D.C., to see it. They marveled at the tall stone tower. It was the tallest building in the world at that time. And it had been built to last, even during an earthquake.

Today, the Washington Monument still stands as a symbol of our nation and a monument to the nation's first president. But major repairs and new safety features are needed to make sure it remains safe in case another earthquake occurs. The building will reopen for tours once it is fully repaired and updated. In the meantime, the most recognizable monument on the Mall is still a beautiful site for celebrations.

The Washington Monument still had its scaffolding in place on July 4, 2013. Even so, it was a perfect place to watch the fireworks.

Check In What parts of the Washington Monument received the most damage from the earthquake?

GENRE **History Article** **Read to find out** what it takes to create a national monument.

The Making of a Memorial

by Hugh Westrup

A champion of liberty. That's how Americans view Thomas Jefferson, one of our nation's founders and the third president of the United States. Jefferson was the main author of the Declaration of Independence, the document that told the British that the American colonies wanted their freedom. His essays and speeches have taught us the importance of independence. It's easy to see why the U.S. Congress approved the creation of a memorial to Jefferson in 1934. But creating the monument was easier said than done. Where would

it be located? What would it look like? These questions and more had to be answered before construction could begin. Congress appointed a group of people to make all of these decisions.

The site they selected had a perfect view of the White House, but it was right in the middle of a grove of cherry trees. This was a problem, because the trees would have to be moved. The city of Tokyo, Japan, had sent the beautiful trees to Washington, D.C., as a gift. Some people were worried that moving them might offend the Japanese. Also, digging up the trees could damage them, and no one wanted the trees to be harmed. In the end, workers did move some of the cherry trees to new locations. Many cherry trees still surround the monument.

Protesters chained themselves to cherry trees in 1938 to try to prevent them from being moved to make way for the memorial.

An Ancient Design

Once the location was picked, it was time to choose the design of the monument. The Jefferson Memorial's designers included **architect** John Russell Pope. He wanted it to look like the ancient Roman Pantheon. The Pantheon had been built 1,800 years earlier in Rome, Italy. The design of the Pantheon features **columns** in the front and a **dome** for a roof. Pope had designed other buildings based on the styles of ancient Greece and Rome.

The Pantheon is a temple to the Roman gods. Until modern times, it had the largest dome (shown at the top) ever built.

Jefferson designed this building at the University of Virginia. He got his inspiration from the Pantheon.

The architect drew plans for the inside and outside of the memorial. These plans are called blueprints, and they show how to construct the building.

Pope and the designers had a good reason to pick this ancient design. Jefferson had been an architect himself and had modeled several buildings on the Pantheon. However, not everyone liked this ancient look. Some argued that a memorial built in the 20th century should look modern, not ancient. They called the planned structure a "misfit" and an "insult to the memory of Thomas Jefferson." But President Franklin D. Roosevelt liked the design. He told the builders to use the ancient design and begin working on the Jefferson Memorial.

The Chrysler Building in New York City was built only a few years before the Jefferson Memorial. Its sleek look shows the modern style of architecture that some would have preferred for the memorial.

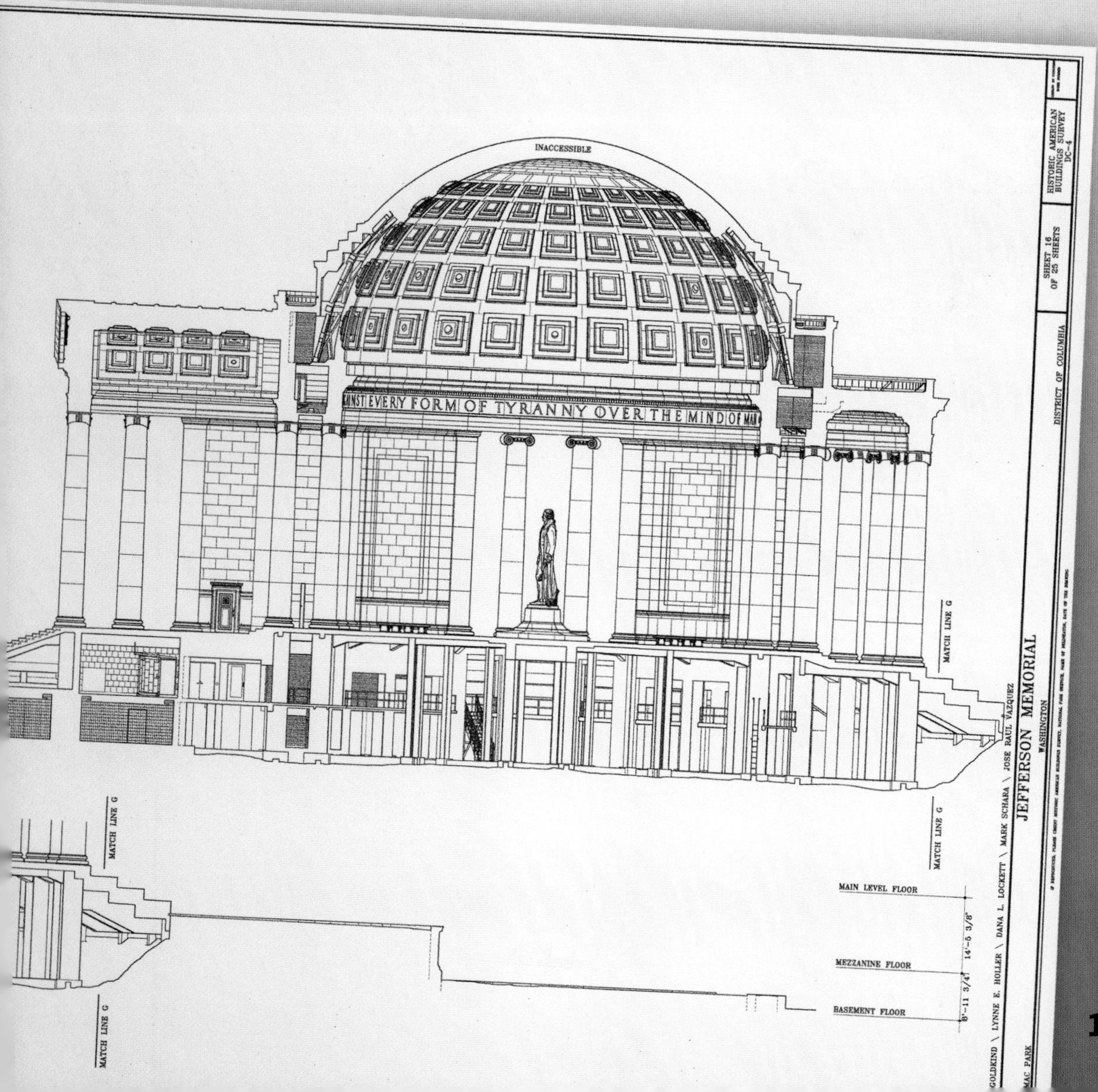

Powerful Words, Powerful Statue

Thomas Jefferson was a famous writer and speaker, and his words carried great power. It made sense to include Jefferson's most important words in his memorial. But which words best showed Jefferson's beliefs? One quotation that was picked came from the second line of the Declaration of Independence:

"We hold these truths to be self-evident: that all men are created equal, that they are endowed by their Creator with certain inalienable rights, among these are life, liberty and the pursuit of happiness . . ."

Those famous words are carved in stone on the inside wall of the memorial. Some people complained about the quotation. Because Jefferson didn't write the document alone, they argued that these words might not really be his.

Four other quotations appear on the inside wall of the monument. They had to be shortened so they would fit and be easier to read. Some people felt the changes meant the carved words were not really what Jefferson said or wrote.

The plan for the memorial called for a tall bronze statue of Thomas Jefferson at its center. But the United States was fighting in a war when the memorial opened in 1943. The nation needed metal to build tanks, airplanes, naval ships, and weapons. So the builders could not use bronze for the statue. Instead, they built a plaster statue and coated it with bronze paint. When the war was over, they replaced the plaster statue with a bronze one that truly honors this great leader.

The National Park Service reports that more than two million people visit the Jefferson Memorial each year.

Check In How does this memorial honor Jefferson's words and deeds?

GENRE Graphic Novel

Read to find out how Abraham Lincoln's character and experiences helped make him a great leader.

HONORING HONEST ABE

by Elizabeth Massie
illustrated by David Harrington

Some people are "larger than life." Abraham Lincoln was one of those people. Lincoln was born a simple country boy, but with hard work, he became a successful lawyer and eventually the 16th president of the United States. His experiences and challenges growing up helped shape the president he would become.

ABE LINCOLN WAS BORN IN KENTUCKY ON FEBRUARY 12, 1809. HIS FAMILY MOVED TO THE INDIANA FRONTIER IN 1816. A FRONTIER IS AN AREA SETTLED BY PEOPLE NEXT TO A WILDERNESS. THERE, THE FAMILY BUILT A CABIN. THEY SURVIVED BY RAISING VEGETABLES AND ANIMALS FOR FOOD.
WHAT A STRONG, HARDWORKING BOY! I IMAGINE HE'LL DO GREAT THINGS WHEN HE GROWS UP.

THOUGH HE RARELY ATTENDED SCHOOL, ABE LOVED TO READ. HE ALMOST ALWAYS CARRIED A BORROWED BOOK WITH HIM. HIS DESIRE TO LEARN HELPED PREPARE HIM FOR HIS LIFE'S CHALLENGES.
THE THINGS I WANT TO KNOW ARE IN BOOKS. MY BEST FRIEND IS THE MAN WHO'LL GET ME A BOOK I HAVEN'T READ.
ABE WORKED FOR NEIGHBORING FARMERS TO MAKE EXTRA MONEY TO HELP HIS FAMILY. ONE JOB WAS SPLITTING WOOD INTO RAILS FOR FENCES. HE WAS SO GOOD AT IT THAT HE GOT THE NICKNAME "RAIL SPLITTER." HE LEARNED THE VALUE OF HARD WORK, WHICH ALSO HELPED PREPARE HIM FOR THE FUTURE.

WHEN ABE WAS 19, HE BUILT A FLATBOAT, WHICH IS A BOAT WITH A FLAT BOTTOM MADE TO CARRY GOODS ALONG A WATERWAY. IN 1828, ABE AND ANOTHER MAN SAILED THE FLATBOAT SOUTH ON THE MISSISSIPPI RIVER TO NEW ORLEANS.
HEAR THAT ROAR? THERE'S ROUGH WATER AHEAD!
PULL HARD, ABE! WE'LL KEEP THIS BOAT AFLOAT!

IT WAS IN NEW ORLEANS THAT ABE SAW A SLAVE MARKET, WHERE SLAVE TRADERS BOUGHT AND SOLD ENSLAVED PEOPLE TO WORK ON PLANTATIONS. A PLANTATION IS A VERY LARGE FARM. ABE WAS ANGRY AND UPSET TO SEE THESE PEOPLE TREATED SO HORRIBLY. THEY WERE BEATEN, CHAINED, AND FORCED TO OBEY THEIR "MASTERS." THIS EXPERIENCE SHAPED ABE'S OPINIONS ABOUT SLAVERY.
THEY'RE SELLING THAT WOMAN TO ONE PLANTATION OWNER AND HER TINY CHILD TO ANOTHER! HOW CAN THIS HAPPEN IN A LAND OF FREEDOM?

WHEN ABE WAS A YOUNG MAN, HE WORKED IN A STORE. ONE DAY HE REALIZED HE'D CHARGED A WOMAN A FEW TOO MANY PENNIES. HE WALKED SEVERAL MILES TO THE WOMAN'S HOME TO RETURN HER PENNIES.
I'M SORRY, MA'AM. I ACCIDENTALLY CHARGED YOU TOO MUCH.
WHY, THANK YOU, ABE. I WISH ALL MERCHANTS WERE AS HONEST AS YOU!
MY RICH NEIGHBOR CLAIMS THAT PART OF MY LAND IS HIS. I DON'T KNOW WHAT TO DO!
IT ISN'T RIGHT THAT YOU'RE HAVING THIS MUCH TROUBLE! LET ME TALK TO THE TOWN COUNCIL ABOUT THIS.
WORKING IN THE STORE GAVE ABE THE CHANCE TO TALK TO HIS NEIGHBORS AND GET TO KNOW THEIR CONCERNS. HEARING PEOPLE'S CONCERNS AND WANTING TO HELP LED ABE TO AN INTEREST IN POLITICS AND LAW.

ABE'S INTEREST IN THE LAW GREW, SO HE DECIDED TO STUDY TO BECOME A LAWYER. HE WORKED AT HIS JOB DURING THE DAY AND STUDIED LAW ON HIS OWN AT NIGHT. HE TRAVELED LONG DISTANCES TO WATCH LAWYERS WORK IN COURT. ABE WORKED AS HARD AT HIS LAW STUDIES AS HE HAD WORKED SPLITTING RAILS.
THERE'S NO WAY I CAN AFFORD LAW SCHOOL. IT'S A GOOD THING JUDGE DRUMMOND LETS ME BORROW HIS BOOKS.

AS A LAWYER, ABE WORKED TO FIND COMMON GROUND BETWEEN PEOPLE WHO HAD DISAGREEMENTS. HE SAW THE ROLE OF A LAWYER AS BEING A PEACEMAKER. THIS VIEW WOULD BE VERY IMPORTANT TO HIM WHEN HE BECAME A POLITICAL LEADER.
CALM DOWN, GENTLEMEN. I'M SURE WE CAN FIND A WORKABLE COMPROMISE.

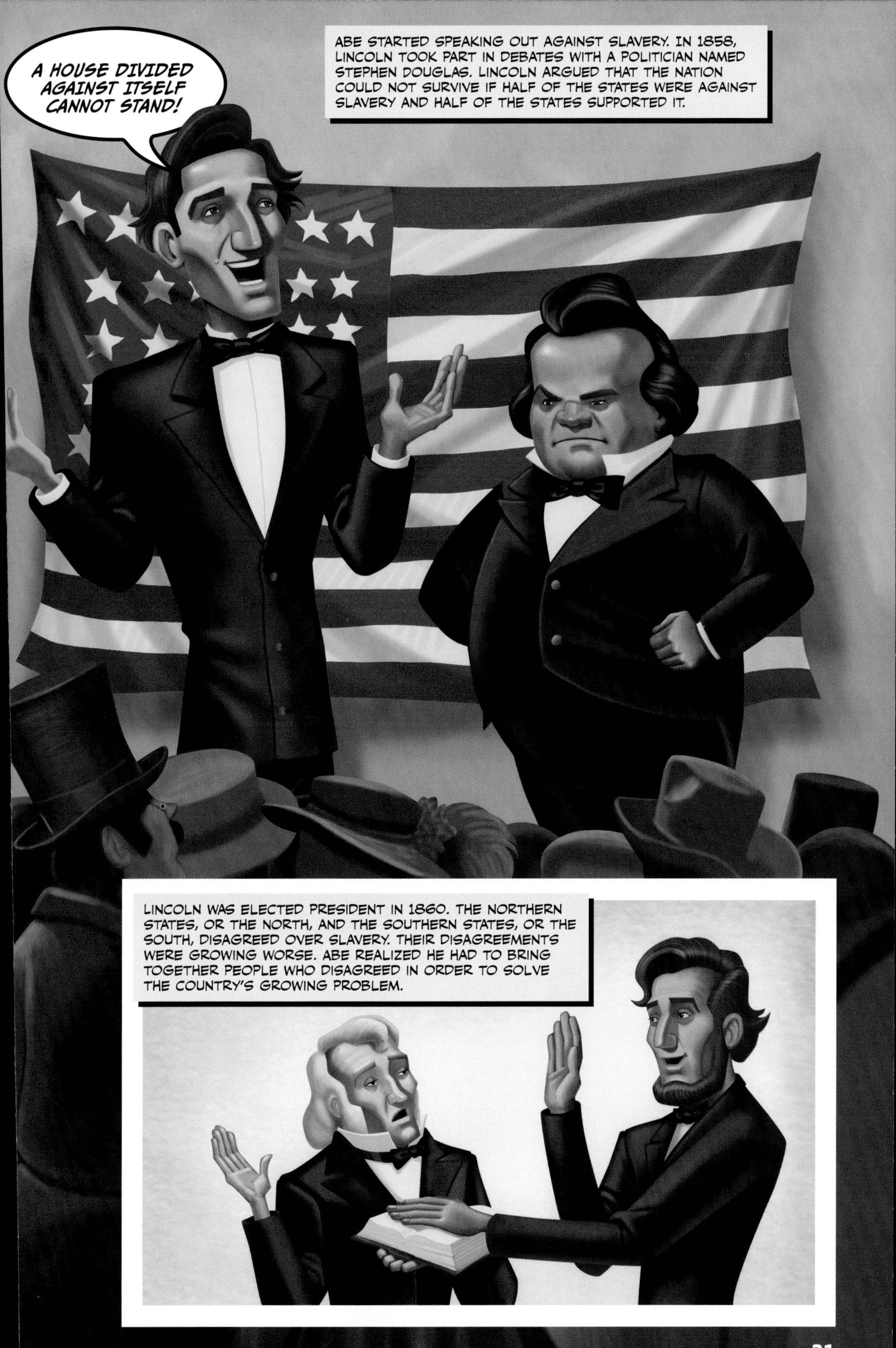
A HOUSE DIVIDED AGAINST ITSELF CANNOT STAND!
ABE STARTED SPEAKING OUT AGAINST SLAVERY. IN 1858, LINCOLN TOOK PART IN DEBATES WITH A POLITICIAN NAMED STEPHEN DOUGLAS. LINCOLN ARGUED THAT THE NATION COULD NOT SURVIVE IF HALF OF THE STATES WERE AGAINST SLAVERY AND HALF OF THE STATES SUPPORTED IT.
LINCOLN WAS ELECTED PRESIDENT IN 1860. THE NORTHERN STATES, OR THE NORTH, AND THE SOUTHERN STATES, OR THE SOUTH, DISAGREED OVER SLAVERY. THEIR DISAGREEMENTS WERE GROWING WORSE. ABE REALIZED HE HAD TO BRING TOGETHER PEOPLE WHO DISAGREED IN ORDER TO SOLVE THE COUNTRY'S GROWING PROBLEM.

SADLY, THE DISAGREEMENTS BETWEEN THE NORTH AND THE SOUTH WERE TOO STRONG. SOUTHERN STATES PROCLAIMED THEMSELVES A SEPARATE NATION. THE CIVIL WAR HAD BEGUN.
I FIGHT FOR THE SOUTH!
I FIGHT FOR THE NORTH!
DURING THE CIVIL WAR, LINCOLN WROTE THE EMANCIPATION PROCLAMATION, WHICH FREED ENSLAVED AFRICAN AMERICANS IN THE SOUTHERN STATES THAT WERE AT WAR WITH THE NORTH. LATER HE LED CONGRESS IN PASSING THE 13TH AMENDMENT TO THE CONSTITUTION. THIS ENDED SLAVERY IN THE ENTIRE UNITED STATES.
IN GIVING FREEDOM TO THE SLAVE, WE GIVE FREEDOM TO THE FREE.

Check In How did Lincoln's early life experiences shape him into a leader of our country?

GENRE Biography

Read to find out about a man whose dream helped change the country.

The Story of a Dream

by Becky Manfredini

He had a dream that all U.S. citizens would have equal rights. He dreamed that the color of their skin or how rich or poor they were wouldn't matter. Dr. Martin Luther King, Jr. led the fight for **civil rights** to make his dream come true.

Dr. King faced threats, violence, and jail time from those who disagreed with him, but he never gave up his fight. He always used peaceful methods. This process was slow, but it was effective.

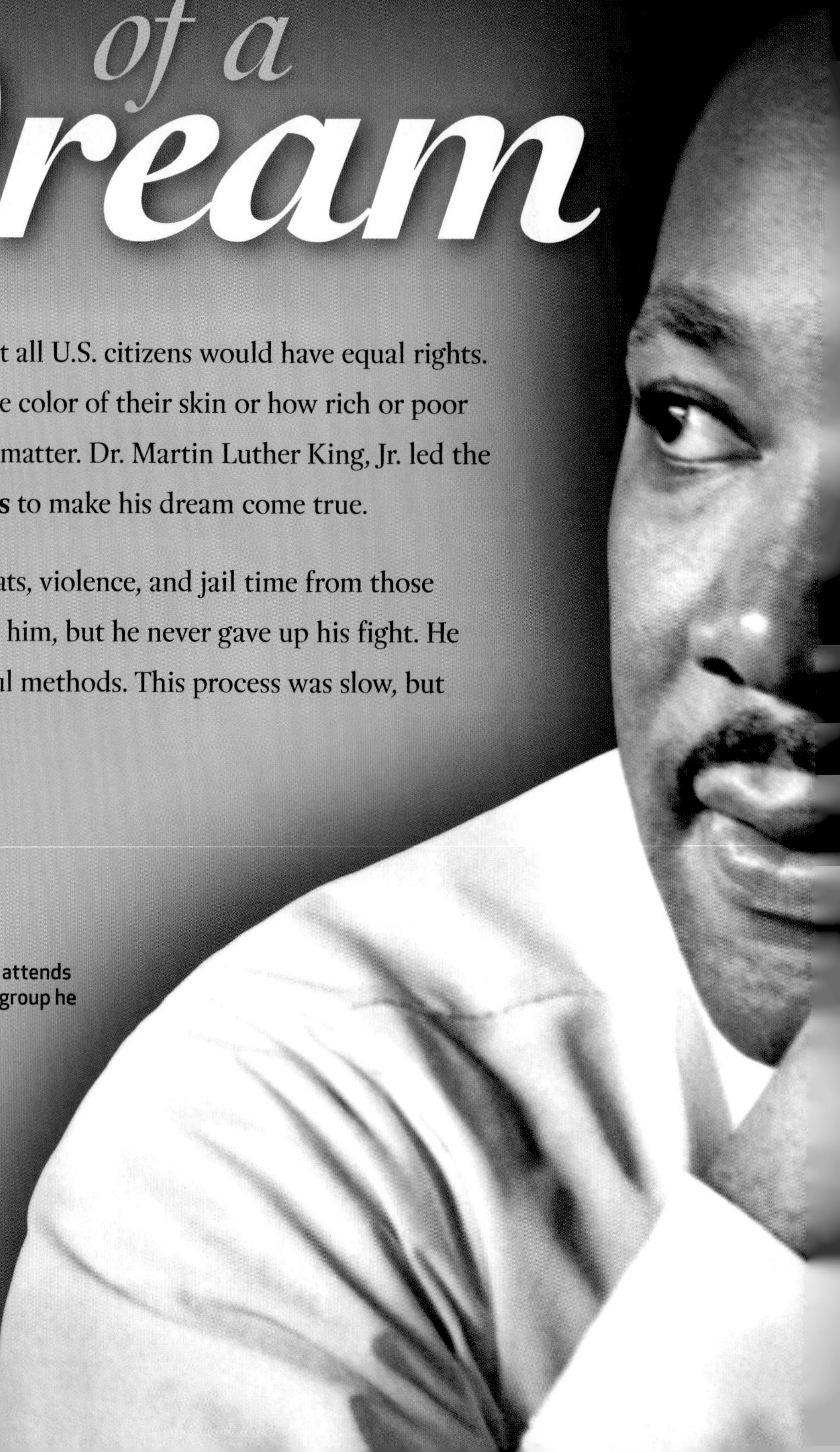

Dr. Martin Luther King, Jr. attends a meeting of a civil rights group he started in the 1950s.

Martin Luther King, Jr. was born on January 15, 1929, in Atlanta, Georgia. His parents, Reverend Martin Luther King, Sr. and Alberta Williams King, provided a happy family life for Martin and his brother and sister.

Young Martin got his first taste of **segregation** at the age of six, when two white friends told him that their parents wouldn't let them play with him. At that time, laws in the southern part of the United States separated black and white citizens in many parts of public life. For example, black and white children could not eat at the same restaurants. They could not drink from the same water fountains. They could not go to the same schools.

Martin was a bright student. He was accepted to Morehouse College, an all-black school, at the age of 15. But he wanted to follow in his father's footsteps. He became a minister before finishing college.

Marching to Freedom

As a minister, Dr. King was determined to fight discrimination, the unfair treatment of people. He preached about equality in his church and began leading peaceful protests throughout the South. His hope was that black and white citizens would have the same rights.

In 1955, another person joined Dr. King's fight against segregation. In Montgomery, Alabama, a bus driver told a black woman named Rosa Parks to give up her seat to a white man. Parks refused to give up her seat, and she was put in jail. Dr. King supported Parks's action and led a bus **boycott**. For a year, African Americans refused to ride the buses in Montgomery. The boycott caused the bus company to lose money. In 1956, the U.S. Supreme Court ordered the city to allow blacks and whites to sit together on buses.

But buses, schools, and stores weren't the only places where civil rights were ignored. In 1870, the 15th Amendment to the U.S. Constitution gave

Dr. King changed our nation by leading peaceful marches. Here, Dr. King and his wife Coretta take part in the March Against Fear in 1966. They walked more than 200 miles from Memphis, Tennessee, to Jackson, Mississippi.

black men the right to vote. Yet many unfair laws remained. These laws made it difficult and even impossible for some African Americans to vote. Some people had to take a reading and writing test before they could register to vote. Poor African Americans were told they had to pay a tax to vote. In 1957, Dr. King held a demonstration in Washington, D.C., that inspired thousands of people to demand equal voting rights.

By 1960, both black and white citizens were working hard to promote civil rights. Dr. King encouraged black college students to have "sit-ins." They sat in whites-only areas in restaurants and refused to leave until they were served. Many restaurants called the police to arrest the protestors. These protests made the national news. People around the country began to see the unfair treatment African Americans faced.

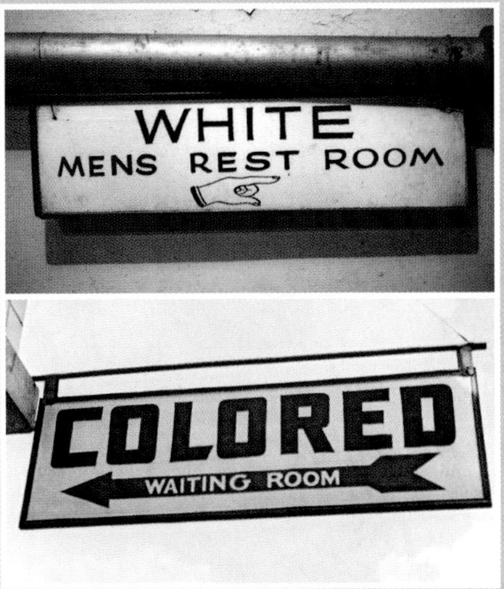

In many places in the South, black and white citizens could not use the same restrooms or waiting areas.

Dr. Martin Luther King, Jr. married Coretta Scott in 1953. The couple lived in Montgomery, Alabama. They had four children, Yolanda, Martin, Dexter, and Bernice.

The Dream Grows

In August of 1963, Dr. King led 250,000 people in the March on Washington for Jobs and Freedom. Thousand of Americans of all races gathered on the National Mall. Civil rights leaders spoke and singers performed. But they were all waiting for Dr. King to speak to them.

He stood at the Lincoln Memorial before the statue of Lincoln, a man whose efforts helped end slavery. Dr. King's powerful voice rose. The crowd grew quiet.

The peaceful March on Washington was broadcast to a national television audience. It brought many Americans face-to-face with the Civil Rights Movement.

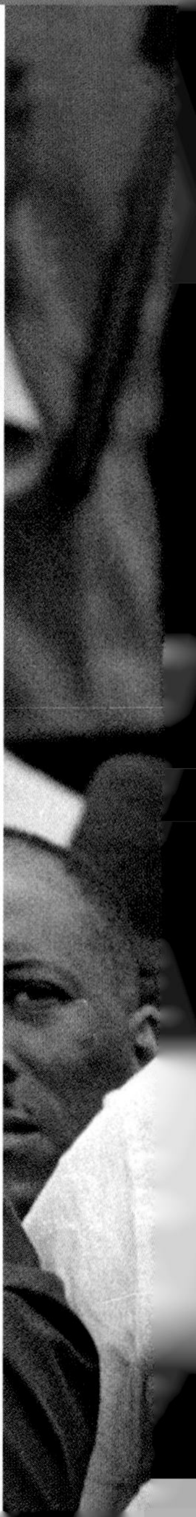

He had prepared a short speech, but Dr. King began to speak from his heart.

Afterwards, Dr. King told graduate student Donald Smith, *"I started out reading the speech . . . the audience response was wonderful that day. . . . And all of a sudden this thing came to me . . . 'I have a dream . . .'"* At that moment, he stopped reading the speech he had prepared. Instead, he talked about his dream for equality. This now-famous address is known as his "I Have a Dream" speech, and his moving words inspired millions to take up the cause of civil rights.

"I Have a Dream" remains one of the most heartfelt and stirring speeches in support of civil rights.

Remember the Dream

At the age of 35, Dr. King became the youngest person to be awarded the Nobel Peace Prize. This honor is given to people who promote peace worldwide. He donated the award money to the Civil Rights Movement and continued seeking his dream. On April 4, 1968, however, Dr. King was shot and killed in Memphis, Tennessee. The nation was shocked by the news and mourned a great loss. But Dr. King's work still inspires people to fight against discrimination.

Today, his dream lives on at the Martin Luther King, Jr. National Memorial in Washington, D.C. It is located near the

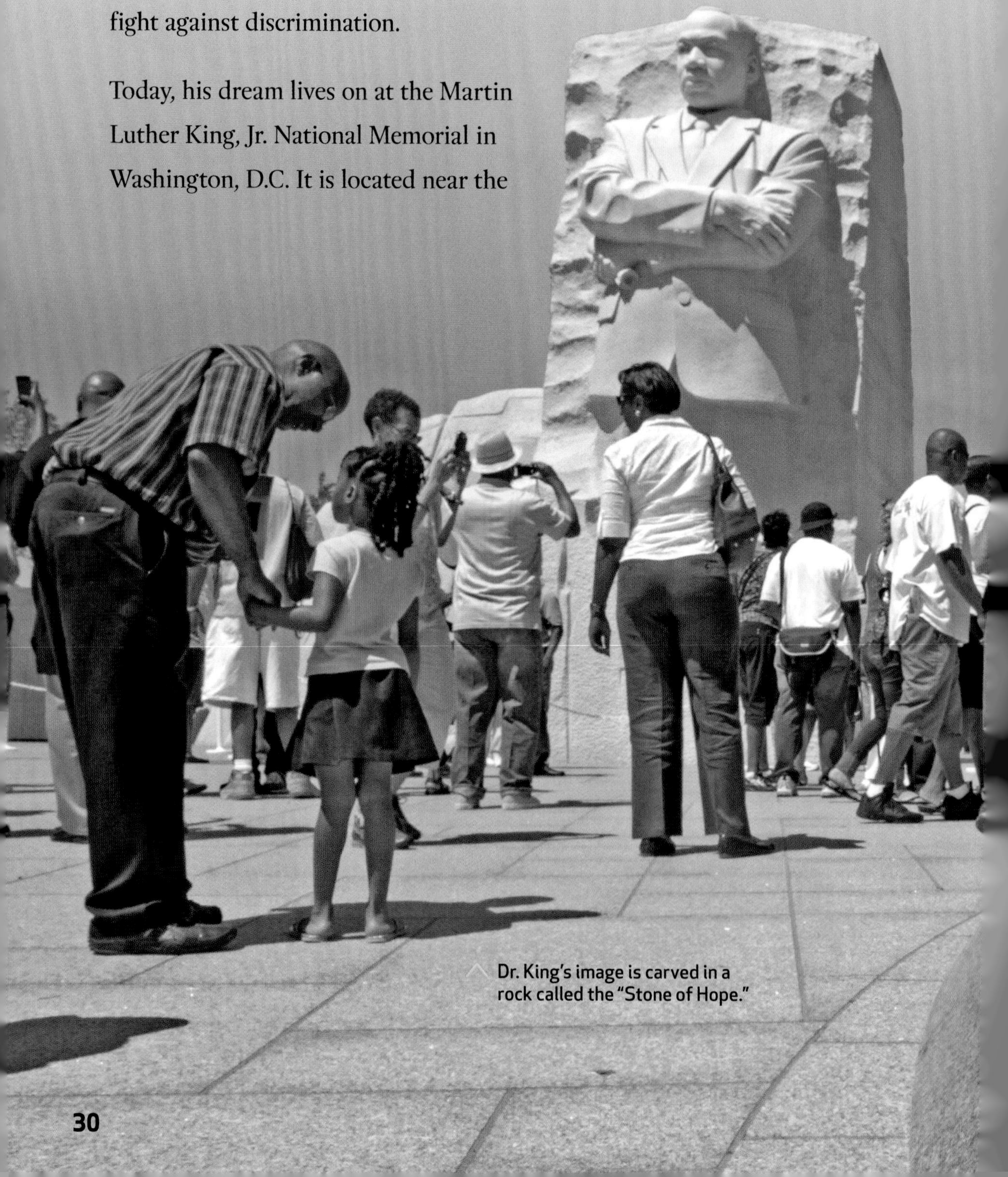

Dr. King's image is carved in a rock called the "Stone of Hope."

Lincoln Memorial, where Dr. King gave his famous speech. The monument features Dr. King's image carved in stone. It looks as if King is coming out of a piece of solid rock. The image of this great leader stands determined and noble.

Dr. King's **legacy** continues to this day. Americans celebrate it every January on Martin Luther King, Jr. Day, a national holiday that honors his life and work. His tireless efforts led to the Civil Rights Act of 1964, which forbids discrimination based on race or gender. A year later, Congress passed the Voting Rights Act of 1965. This law removed the unfair practices that had kept African Americans from being able to vote. Thanks to Dr. King, we are closer than ever to true civil rights for all Americans.

> *"If you can't fly then run, if you can't run then walk, if you can't walk then crawl, but whatever you do you have to keep moving forward."* —DR. MARTIN LUTHER KING, JR.

Check In How did Dr. Martin Luther King, Jr. use peaceful measures to fight for civil rights?

Discuss

1. What connections can you make among the five selections in this book? How are the selections related?

2. What is a symbol of liberty? How are the monuments on the National Mall symbols of liberty? Can you think of any others?

3. What were some of Abraham Lincoln's personal qualities that made him a great leader?

4. Dr. Martin Luther King, Jr. dreamed of equality and justice for all Americans. In your opinion, has this dream come true? Explain your answer.

5. What else do you want to know about the famous leaders from our past who inspired these monuments? How can you find out more?